For those who know how difficult it is to exist,
and who choose to continue existing anyway.

The world is better with you here.

Published by Stanchion Books, LLC

StanchionZine.com

Edited by Katie Schmeling

Cover design by Jeff Bogle

Cover photograph by Lynne Schmidt

ISBN: 979-8-88862-255-1

The Unaccounted For Circles Of Hell

Lynne Schmidt

STANCHION

Dante Was Wrong

In Dante's Divine Comedy,
he proposed there are nine circles of hell
and claimed to have walked through each.

He forgot to mention
      the circle where your clothes make you a victim
      and your stomach is the assailant.

      The circle of hell reserved for
      watching your favorite aunt lose her memory.

      The circle when the man you love marries someone else.

      The circle of hell where your mother
      and your sisters can't be in the same room,
      and your entire family sees you as the skeleton you were
      ten years ago still hanging in the closet by a noose.

He forgot to mention the circle reserved for
      not making it in time for a visit before your friend dies,
      missing your babcia's last breath,
      your uncle dying the day you're supposed to visit,
      and your aunt becoming a ballerina with the most beautiful
performance to convince us she's fine.

He forgot to mention
      the circle where you wait on a hospital floor for a diagnosis
and how you sink into another
      when you're given the word, *terminal.*

Apparently
      Dante never experienced the circle of hell
      reserved for the phone ringing, and ringing,

      and your sister telling you a heart stopped working.

And another didn't survive the accident.

He never experienced the level reserved
for when your role shifts
        and now you break the news of a passing
        to your sister, and listen to her gasping for air
        a thousand miles away.

No one addresses the spaces in hell
for the aftermath of grief
the way your bones continue to operate
but your chest hollows out.

So how many circles of hell
are there really?

Because I know even I'm not able to list them all.

        I just live in them.

Circle 10
Sexual Assault

Necrophilia
(After Taking Off Emily Dickinson's Clothes)

Years after you're dead,
they will still spend time trying to remove your dress,
still spend time exploring your corpse as it lays still,
because though you should have the liberty to rest in peace,
they feel entitled to their pieces of your body, still.

In life,
I'm sure you would have written about them,
demolished them like a building,
would have bitten them with your teeth,
taken out chunks of skin and swallowed them whole.

They attack you in death,
because here, you won't scream,
won't breathe,
won't be able to defend yourself
like the drunk women they find behind dumpsters.

But she was allowed to be drunk,
and you are allowed to be dead.

They will tell us that when it happens,
you are "a little wide eyed,"
as they strip you down,
mistaking flesh decayed corpse sockets
for eyes.

The men will praise this act of necrophilia,
offer awards and congratulations on the accomplishment,
see the beauty in violating yet another woman,
the perceived gentleness of the unbuttoning.

And the women will realize
living a real-time horror story,
that even in death,
we still aren't safe from being raped.

Lies I Tell Myself

I often say that if a stranger were to
_______________ that they would catch
an elbow to the face.
That they would get throat punched.
That I would defend myself.

I have often baffled when friends have said,
"I was too shocked to respond,"
because I tell myself, I am always ready.

But the truth is,
a few years back,
my partner invited me to his staff party.

While he went to get us some food,
I stood in line to get a drink.

And when a drunk stranger stumbled up to me,
clutched a breast in each hand,
and smiled at me

I just stood there,
shaking.

When They Become Husbands

I wonder if his wife remembers
his rampage in undergrad -
the moment he strutted out of the bathroom
and proclaimed his conquest of a new transfer
and received a line of high fives like
the Friday night football tunnel.

If he ever told his wife
how this young girl,
scrambling for friends,
came out of the bathroom
too inebriated to walk, fell
like a stage dive into hands that
were willing to high five him,
but fail to catch her.

Stitches from a wall on her face,
a souvenir, just above her eyebrow.

If he told his wife,
before they had children
and she posted all of their happy pictures together,
him and his infant daughter,
how many scars
he gave the other girls in the dorm.

Victory And Bruises

Sometimes I think about the rape,
my wooden thighs splitting open with
the lightning burn as he tried to push in,
how my sister would later tell me that sometimes,
if you really don't want it,
muscles will clench so tightly
they turn to stone.

I wanted the clenching of my jaw
to be a red flare for someone to come
get me out of the bed of the purple truck.

I understood why some women scream from pain,
why some men cover their mouths.

When finished,
because things don't slide on dry and raw land,
he drove me home.

In the morning, he said he was sorry.

His arm harbored a blue-green algae bloom,
large enough that when we all went to Chinese Buffet,
friends asked how he got it.

And he said as casually as he took my underpants off,
I hit it on something.

But I could tell you the exact way he moved,
how his flesh collided with the metal of the truck,
how he said *Ouch* before I did.

And how that bruise looked like victory to me.

Circle 11
Violence Against Women

The Day After She Goes Missing

They find her body the day after
the missing-person alert is released.

The newspapers write about how her husband was
    such a loving man -
        he donated money, time, energy.
        He was an all-star student and they
        were high school sweethearts.
They smiled in every one of their pictures on social media.

And while the papers are so busy glamorizing this man
with his wife's blood still wet on his hands,
they will fail to report the outbursts,
    the screaming matches,
    the fists through walls,
    fists near faces,
    bruises on bodies covered by clothes -
the things that eclipse what a good man is.

They won't tell us about the hospital visits,
the desperation to get away,
the dancing on eggshells to make sure everything is perfect
the apologies and promises of
    "I swear, I'll change.
        This will never happen again."
And the want to believe it.

After they find her body,
the newspapers will only tell us of the great man

and the woman who went back to him.

Autopsy

After she's dead,
they'll release the details they deem important:

She is missing.
There was a fight.
Police were involved.
It was her fault, she was crazy,
she was crying, who could act like that?

They will look for her,
then tell us where they found her.

They will talk about a person of interest,
who by then has disappeared into the wilderness.
Eventually they will release
the cause of death.

They will not tell us rope or bare hands,
they'll leave out the look in his eyes as the light left hers,
they will use the single word: strangulation,
without using the words suspect, foul play, domestic abuse,
how many women die at the literal hands of their male partners,
how many go missing.

And then,
because what is a woman if not pregnant,
they will tell us

the contents of her uterus
were empty.

Richmond Park

My sister's husband tells her to stop running at the park.
I think he's trying to control her,
like that time she said she had to ask permission to get a tattoo.

He says it isn't safe.
She says, she's been running there for months.

Eventually, she relents and finds a different route.

I get the call two days later,
her voice is shaking when she says they found a body,
a runner, same hair color, same height, similar clothes,
a woman in the same running shoes.

She tells me
she ran the trail the day before.

Circle 12
Attacks on Reproductive Rights

When There Is A Decision To Be Made

After she marries,
every time my sister calls
I answer with, *Hi - are you pregnant yet?*

For months, she chuckles
and tells me no.

One day after I answer,
she is quiet for so long,

I know the answer before she says yes.

Consequences

Remember:
according to the Bible
pregnancy
is a punishment

not a blessing.
Remember:
Eve ate the fruit
committed the sin

and God is a jealous
and vengeful God.
And a man must have written
the Bible.

Must have
seen his child
ripped from
between his wife's
or mistress's legs
must have said

I have caused this pain
look what I can do!

Remember:
he will someday say
I dictate this pregnancy
you have

no choice.

My Body As A Gun

If my vagina was the cold metallic barrel,
my cervix the muzzle,
my uterus the magazine well,
ovaries as bullets,
would you trust me
to know when to pull the trigger?

What if I forgot the safety?
What if there were only so many bullets?

What would it take for you
to trust me with my own gun?

Circle 13
Gun Violence

When The News Reads, "School Shooting In Michigan"

I scramble for the link so the town is named.
I didn't call my sister today
because I knew she would be teaching,
and when the final bell rang,
collecting her children from another school.

At some point, I texted,
a message floating with no response.

The time it takes from link click to page load
is enough time to count every fucking star
in the galaxy.

When I read Oxford, I selfishly exhale
because my family is safe
while three prepare for a funeral.

The dead include a 14-year-old,
the same age as my oldest niece,
the one I didn't even get to hug the last time
I was in the state because she was sick
and I could not afford transmission.

Some of the students post videos on Tik-Tok
of the shooter trying to enter the classroom.
The video keeps rolling and catches
the small squeaks of stifled shrieks
as bodies pour like smoke out of the window
running across the graveyard of snow
to the open door
where someone greets,

"You're safe now,
slow down."

Two Blocks Away

I could walk to the stop sign nearest my apartment,
turn around and see two blocks down the street.

The first block holds the rule:
if the dogs poop between here and there,
we use the scoop. It's so close and
we don't want to waste a plastic bag.

        At the second block, there are baseball fields.

                When snowstorms come,
            my roommate and I walk down,
                    pick up the dogs,
                      hop the fence,
     and let them run until tired or cold,
                      the whole time,
                our apartment in view,
          close enough to walk back to.

Last night,
a gunman starts his massacre
fifteen minutes from my sister.

When I tell my roommate,
he says fifteen minutes
is still pretty far on foot.

        The gunman ended the night
      two blocks away from my sister.

       A self-inflicted gunshot wound.
        A bang close enough,
          it rang in her ears.

Maroon Dodge Ram
For Abraham

with five golf ball sized bullet holes
blasting through the driver's side window.

Call a tow company in the morning
peel the truck off the street
once the body is cold in the morgue.

Call it gang violence.
Talk about the people
drinking champagne in the streets.

Call it drug deals, remind the public
he was throwing heroin out of his window
before the police arrived.

Show the photos of the spiderwebs in the glass,
get close enough you're able to count the holes
like a game of connect the dots.

Ensure the detachment from human,
include every detail of all the horrible things he did
since he started dealing drugs at the age of thirteen.

Show the holes in the glass.

Be careful to not show the blood stains.

Because if you do,
you might have to tell the public he was human, too.

The photos don't show a few years ago,
the man who drove the truck
seeing his one-hundred-and-twenty-pound neighbor
trying to bring their couch up the stairs,

it falling from their hands,
and him offering to help.

The photos don't show
for the better part of two years,
the neighbor looked in a parking spot
to see if the Maroon Dodge Ram was parked
in the hopes of saying
Hi, how was your day?

The photos just show the bullet holes
in the driver's side of the truck.

Not the neighbor sitting on their couch,
seeing the photos in the news, and crying.

Texts The Day Of An Active Shooter

You left, right? You're not in the LA area?
You're safe?
What happened?
We were at the bowling alley.
I tied a kids arm off.
He was bleeding a lot.
I hid my kids under a desk and barricaded a door with another
mom.
What in the actual fuck.
Jesus Christ this world is insane.
I'm so sorry this has happened near you.
Hey! Are you near Lewiston, Maine right now?
I saw on the news there is an active shooter in that area right now.
Are you ok and are you safe?
Yes we are all safe.
And I still love you, even when you hate me.
Hey, boss. How're you holding up?
I saw your tweet about stories rolling in from friends of friends.
I remember having the same experience after Pulse ...
just wanted to check on you, see if you need anything.
Yes, her husband was called in
he's the supply room manager
they needed all the body bags he had
because they have 16 and are still getting more.
My closest friends husband was shot.
I wish he just killed himself instead of this shit.
I literally think I might throw up.
They haven't found him yet.
They haven't found him yet.
They haven't found him yet.
Are you safe?
Are you okay?

Circle 14
Body Image & Eating Disorders

Dysmorphia

He takes a picture
of a girl on a lake
and a dog beside her.

And all I see is the way the sun touches her skin.

It's not gentle,
sunlight through the tangle of trees.

It's a sledgehammer against dry wall
because she isn't sitting straight
which causes the excess to push together,
an accordion of skin
in a way that literally no other person but me
would see.

Where straight lines should live
there is a curve
and while most people who would view the photo
would see the dog,
the lake,
a smiling girl,
the contrast of light,
I see the sunlight on too much skin.

So he hands me my phone back
and what should be a treasured moment
gets deleted.

The Perfect Dress

I chose it
the way most people browse a clothing catalog--
flipping through the first three pages
and deciding that dress hurts your teeth
and that one wouldn't fit right either.

Until finally the perfect one stared back at me,
wax pages glistening in sunlight.

I'd found the perfect one,
submitted something like a credit card,
and cashed out with:
      no fat reserves left,
      a hospitalization placement,
      protein in my urine,
a partner pausing as he takes my shirt off, saying,
'I'll always find you attractive,
…but you need to eat.'

I found the perfect dress
and decided to put it on
because it would cover all my defects.

It would make me pretty.
It would keep me thin.
I would dazzle when I turned this way and that.
When I looked in the mirror
I could see someone I recognized.

I slipped the dress on.
Its silk fabric wrapping around my body.

But it was tighter than I imagined.

When I exhaled, my stomach touched the edges.

I learned to take shallow breaths.
I learned to stand up straighter.
I learned to eat with larger spaces in between.
To ask boys not to touch my stomach if I'm sitting down.

And though they call it remission
once you put this dress on,
there aren't enough zippers in the world
to pull you back out.

Birthing And Raising My Anorexia

When it's time for show and tell,
the teacher shows our baby pictures.
When she gets to mine,
she announces to the class that I was
"a fat baby" and am "still fat now."

In sixth grade, before going out to play,
I get into the tool cabinet,
extract the duct tape and wrap a corset
around my eighty-pound body.
When it was my turn for kick ball, I could not
breathe, or move without the adhesive trying to
pull my skin. Later that night, as I peeled it off,
I bled, skin coming away like stickers on notebook paper,
residue and adhesive that takes weeks to wash away.

The following year, I am invited to
a twenty-four hour food fast with a church.
It is the first time my stomach feels hollow.
I learn I can still play volleyball without passing out.
When I come home, I spend some time eating
three baby carrots for breakfast, and a handful of
jellybeans for lunch. I skip dinner and my skin
feels like paper, like maybe I can float away in the
next storm.

After school, Chad and I play basketball.
He tells me Jodi, the blond girl with wrist bones
like a swiss-army knife, is too small, so delicate,
she looks like she needs to eat.
He tells me, he likes my body,
the one with meat on the bones – and I wonder

if there is still too much meat, like maybe
I should be fragile, too.

Sophomore year, the cross-country team sits
in a circle to stretch. Jackie, who looks like Jodi,
is in a sports bra and when she leans forward to touch
her feet, her stomach does not bulge, does not
ripple like cottage cheese.

The summer my sister graduates,
she says she invites our father to her party
because he'll hopefully give her money.
I go with her to greet the man we haven't seen
since his custody was revoked years ago.
The first thing he says to me,
Wow, your face really filled out.

I buy my prom dress the morning of the event.
I joke to my friends that I procrastinated. The reality is
for weeks prior, I sat in the dressing room,
over fifty different dresses saying
my face is the size of a dinner plate,
my hips threaten their tightly sewn seams,
my shoulders might as well be a cardboard box.
The zipper does not slide, it cries.
The dress I choose has a built-in corset,
and if I cannot breathe,
I cannot test the seams.

In college, I eat.
Freshmen year I weigh the most I have ever weighed.
Senior year, I weigh the least I have ever weighed.

My jeans require a belt.
My favorite strapless dress slides off me.
My shirt never touches my stomach.
The hospital tells me there are no fat reserves left,
but I can still feel the meat on my bones,
see the richness in my cheeks.

Years later, I rename my Anorexia, Remission.
She tells me the muffin top looks great,
dares me to run in a sports bra again.
She cheers me on for so long that
I believe I am recovered.

Until one day,
Andrew tells a story about a girl
who is five-two, one hundred pounds,
and my body says,

I can be a hundred pounds if I start now.

An Ode To The COVID Weight I Gained

Cheers to the extra IPAs,
and the two weeks straight of getting high
and eating everything in sight.

Cheers to the mimosas,
the bags of Spicy Nacho Doritos,
the Sour Patch Kids,

and the scale saying
this is the heaviest you have ever been.
Cheers to my jeans not fitting,

and a year of sweatpants instead.
Cheers to trying to force comfort
into a body that has only ever felt

like violation and inconvenience.
Here is to the knowledge,
that my body not only survived

a pandemic,
but had the audacity to expand beyond
anything I have known.

And cheers to me,
for still taking my shirt off at the ocean,
and for trying to love it.

Circle 15
Being LGBTQ+

When It Happens At Work

The day the girls corner Jenna on the sales floor,
she is alone.

Jenna with the short hair,
Jenna who watches Glee,

Jenna, the sweet girl who
sometimes watches my dog for me.

Their words tackle her like a linebacker,
swallow her like the ocean surrounding the island we live on.

When she tells us later that night,
that she hid in the bathroom and cried,

I am raging.
I do not know that I am queer yet.

We tell Jenna we love her,
we tell Jenna, we are here.

And Jenna looks up and says,
I wish, so much, that being gay was a choice.

Because I wouldn't wish this on anyone.

The New Binary
After Phil Kaye

Cutting off my fingertips so they can't hold the box you try to place me in, but still trying to convince you that I am *a lady*, but also cringing when you say you'll carry the heavy stuff down the stairs for me, but thankful because my shoulder surgery didn't heal right, but I swear to God I'm strong, but I am also a victim to my body, but an even worse victim to my heart, who never fucking learns, but you make me blush, but you call me things like girl, and lady, but I am and am not.

What Happens Before You Know Who You Are

The word *dyke* falls out of your co-workers' mouth
like spit up, splattering across everyone who's present.

You laugh because they laugh.

You laugh, because if
you're laughing at them
laughing at you,
it can't hurt, right?

After months
the joke stops being funny,
because it evolves rather than stops.

The day you are in the front page of the newspaper
for helping rehabilitate endangered sea turtles,
you are thrilled.

Until your co-workers cut your face out of the article,
taping it to their tip jar with a quote bubble
misgendering you as "Steve."

Your manager will refuse to take it down.
He will tell you it's just a joke and
"They're just having fun."

Years later, after the Pulse shooting,
you find yourself in Congress Square for the memorial.
You do not know why you need to be there,
just that you do.

You tell your friends you are there for them,
hug them, offer support.

You do not know that you, too,

have been targeted.

The first woman you will have a crush on is named Karen,
and your hands will shake when she buys you a beer.

You will spend years wondering
what it would have been like to kiss her.

Circle 16
Capitalism

Rest Is A Luxury

I remember the time I worked four jobs in Maine
and three jobs in North Carolina
and cried when considering what to eat
but making sure my dog was fed.

I remember working from 6am to 2am
Repeat
Repeat
And missing two days of work because I couldn't
remember what day it was.

When I moved to go to school,
my aunt put $1,000 in my hands and told me
"Pay me back when you're able."

A semester later, I was nearly kicked out of undergrad
because I could not pay the tuition bill.

I remember breaking into houses
to have somewhere warm to sleep that November.

I went to work the day after my abortion.
And worked the day after my knee surgery.

My aunt died ten years after she loaned me money.
I was never able to pay her back.

I tell people to prioritize rest now.

But believe me,
I know that rest is a luxury many can't afford.

Still Life In A Capitalist Nightmare

The therapist is ugly crying on the floor,
with her dog's body twisting in front of her,
neck arched so far backward she fears it may snap.

The dog's urine sprays like a hose
amid convulsions on the carpet.

The therapist screams *Help!* to her roommate,
who yells back, *What do you want?*
and she sobs, *Kyla is having a seizure, get towels.*

The therapist strokes the brown dog's fur
and tell her *it's okay,*
it's alright.

As Kyla comes to,
she rests her head in her person's hands,
as though her person is the only light
that guided her through,
and the therapist cries harder.

There is no sick-time left.
No PTO accrual.

So in ten minutes,
I am supposed to dry my eyes,
return to my office,
and welcome the next patient
with a smile.

Circle 17
Animal Abuse

I Cannot Save Them All
For Shaindel Beers

My friend runs the social media account for an animal rescue,
and she posts about dumped kittens,
abandoned dogs, malnourished puppies.

In some cases, the bones are sticking out,
eye sockets ruptured and infected.
In others, no matter how cute or sweet,
they cannot be saved.

It is hard to exist in this world
of torture, abandonment, and death.
It is hard to know that likely, someone who looks like me,
who has hands like me,
has caused this level of hurt.

Once, she posted about the dogs who died in the fire,
and having to ask for a photo of the bodies,
so she could find an appropriately sized box,
and the owners did not have to deal with this task.

A friend once asked me
how I stomach all this rage,
all this grief, and I told her,
the pets I own are rescues.

I do my best to ensure they are safe
and fed, and loved.
On the days I read a horror story,
we go out for pup cups in honor of them.

And this - this is the best I can do:
care for mine, when I cannot save the others.

Patches

I met her in a Wal Mart parking lot
and fell in love as children do.
I begged and pleaded and won.
We put her tiny body in the car,
and my sister told me I was selfish and stupid.

My father chained her to a doghouse in Michigan.
Said she was never allowed in the house.

She spent summer, fall, winter, spring in a poorly insulated stand,
no toys, cheap food, life on a fifteen-foot chain
waiting for someone to love her.

When I came out to visit
she jumped on me,
and because I was too young
to understand the desperation of loneliness,
I left her.

My father lost the right to see his children,
and when my mother got full custody,
Patches stayed chained to her doghouse.

Years later, I found out
the one winter she was let inside
she ate rat poison and died.

This is how I learned to care for dogs.

This is why when the time comes
and I find an outside dog
who might enjoy the inside,
I open the door.

An Ode To The Now Vs Then Rescue Photo

The day you come home with me,
you cower, tucking yourself so small,
I bite back tears and tell you,
I'm so sorry for what happened.

When I kneel down
like a prayer, soft and gentle,
offering the palms of my hands,
you slowly come to me.

I am cautious, careful to move
at a fraction of the speed I would move
with my dogs.

The first month,
you run from people on our walkies.
You don't know how to play with toys,
how to sleep on a bed.

When we give you a bath,
the grime and dirt flows down the drain,
covering the white bathtub,
like a coloring book.

The first time you approach a stranger to say hi,
I nearly sob because you trust,
somehow, I will keep you safe.

When I come home,
you jump into my arms now.
When we go to bed at night,
your face rests beside mine on the pillow.

Circle 18
Child Abuse & Neglect

The Kind Of Man My Father Is

The metal snaps against wood
loud enough we pause the TV.

The three of us go over to the trap and
I pray for quick death, a false alarm.

Instead, my sisters and I
find a mouse caught,

jaw broken, back paws
frantically kicking at the metal arm crushing it.

My bone marrow wants to free him,
wants to put warning signals around the traps for the others.

Our father marches in,
my sisters and I freeze before scurrying to the couch.

I keep my eyes on the TV
careful not to watch what happens behind me.

He picks up the trap, struggling mouse
and all, walks to the wood stove.

With no more emotion
than putting another log on the fire,

my father opens the door
lifts the metal arm.

And I can still hear the mouse screaming.

Starting At Three

My therapist asks when it started,
and
did I ever blame myself?

I laugh and say,
I was three,
and
I probably deserved it.

My therapist asks
how old my nieces
and
nephew are now.

I don't answer.

She asks if they're around the same age
and
I shrug and answer,
Close enough.

My therapist asks
how I would react if my sister
did to them what our parents did to us.

My therapist asks
if there is anything they could do to
as I said, *deserve it*.

My therapist asks,
if there is no way they could deserve it
how could I have?

Rite Of Passage

My sisters knew how to ride a bike.
During summer, they would pedal up and down the road
with me watching after them until it was time to go inside.

I had training wheels until I didn't,
the expectation that some adult would swoop in
and cheer for me as I scraped my knees.

Only, the adults never put their bottles down long enough
to push me forward. And so one day
as the summer fire roared

I mounted the bike
and struggled to keep my balance
falling over like a drunk.

My father laughed between sips,
You're doing that the hard way
but he never bothered to teach me the easy way.

Car Crash And Broken Glass

Years later, my sister tells me
about the accident she walked away from.

The one where in the morning
a friend took me to look at the carnage:

windshield concaved on metal,
police saying no one should have survived.

I hollowed out the space in my chest
a silent prayer of thanks that my sister is still here.

When we circle back to it, she tells me
of coming home that night, of calling our mother.

How our mother demanded,
If you're fine, why are you calling? then hung up.

and how my sister spent the night picking glass out of her hair.

Circle 19
Death

Buddy System

When the snow gets deep
the rule is
if you choose to go into the trees
you stay within eyesight of your buddy.

> And so we go,
> eyeline like holding hands
> existing in this wonderland together.

> We careen around trees like car accidents
> near misses and drunken nights.
> For once I keep up.

> Which is funny,
> because the race ended three years ago.

The reason for the buddy system
is so if you disappear
under a fresh drift
your buddy digs you out
on their hands and knees
while you wait for oxygen.

I have been waiting for him
to give me permission
to breathe
since we met
and he stole all the air in the universe.

Suddenly, he falls.
I wait several moments to ensure he can get up,
that he doesn't need me.

He rises, he brushes himself off.
He smiles at me,

and I convince myself that my legs shake
because they are tired.

Still, I am careful to not come closer
than eyesight.

He is still a lion, and I am still a lamb.

At the bottom of the mountain
he calls her,
tells her about his fall.

When she asks if he was alone
he looks at me
and says yes.

The Value Of A Photo

Forever etched in whatever glossy printed 4x6 frame allows,
we sit at a table after the Great Falls Brew Fest.

We are both smiling,
me open mouth, teeth showing.

His tight lipped and reserved.
Our arms wrapped around each other,

faces pressed close together like ink on paper.
My cheeks flushed with the remnants of the beers

we spent all day drinking.
He wears a royal blue jersey of some sort,

the same kind he always wore at the mountain.
I am wearing a new Baxter hoodie.

But my dog is not dead yet.
And he is not dead yet.

As of yesterday,
he has been dead for four years.

Time will erode this day from my memory
like a photo crumpled and folded,

sharp image turning back to blank slate.
As it stands, I can no longer remember

our conversation that sunny afternoon.
But if I keep this picture safe,

if I frame it,
we will forever be sitting beside each other,
slightly buzzed and smiling.

Resurrection
For Kellie Lynne Wheeler

I come each year because
I know you'll arrive soon.
And sure enough there you are
in the driveway,

pushing in the clutch,
letting the gas out,
moving the vehicle forward.

I'm not sure when you'll finish
learning to drive a stick-shift,
not sure if you've seen that I've parked,
so I swallow, take a deep breath,
and exit my car.

I meet your mother on the porch,
take her small body in my arms,
and hug her for as long as she lets me
before she guides me to the wicker chairs.

We both know you'll be here soon,
so we're not really sure how to proceed.
We fill the space with banal updates - work, family, writing.

It takes less than ten minutes
before you make your way up the stairs
and settle into a cushioned loveseat,
near your mother and me.

Your mouth stays closed,
a silent spectator,
observing the interaction,
as we continue the conversation.

You are wearing Kara's black jacket,
your thick brown hair is straight.
I want to touch you,
but you sit just out of reach.

Your mother talks about our friendship,
her apprehension because my mother was gone so frequently,
and we were so young, and teenage,
and god knows what teens do when unsupervised.

Your mother says she worried,
about what we could do with all our free time,
stories spinning in her mind of drunk and dangerous adventures.

I tell her about the times we played softball in the yard
because I did poorly in a game,
and you didn't mind practicing with me.

Your mother says,
"I never heard that story before,"
then offers me one of hers in trade.

I could live in this moment,
crack apart the ripples in time,
crawl inside your mother's memory,
and take up residence there.

Because too soon,
the conversation ends,
and you
are dead again.

When You Become A Snowflake
For Joe McMenimen

When the snow finally comes this year,
I collect each flake in a jar,
combing through the frozen varieties,
trying to find you.
Frantic not to lose a single one,
I collect the entirety of Maine's precipitation.
After six years of each snow-covered morning and
your grumpy greeting,
there are only two things you must have become.
And so I search, waiting for your legs to emerge
from a single flake, your eyes to roll when you see me,
because you are supposed to be resting
and I've annoyed you once again,
waiting for your half smile a gruff voice to say hello
before saying *very good* and leaving again.
But –
I am not sure you decided to visit during this storm.
It makes sense – you always liked to make an entrance.

If You're Still Here
For Guy Pomerleau

We talk about the future
things written out in contracts so they will happen
things where the date and time haven't quite been established but
there's still hope they will come to life.

And then you ask me to read to you.
I say I don't have any poems on me.
If you're still here when the book comes out,
I will.

I'll show you the cover with the pages I created
I'll show you the universe of planets, stars, galaxies
I'll read to you
anything you want next time
if you're still here
to listen.

But just in case you're not,
just in case I take too long between this time
and next time,
here's a hug
six words,
one sentence repeated,
and a promise that lingers somewhere near limbo -

If you're still here
I promise to come back.

Winter Solstice
For Eben Dingman

By the time your name
has made headlines
they have already pulled your body
from the wreckage.

Comments pour in-
condolences mixed with
seasons greetings
and collective grief.

Your family will learn
their first Christmas
without you.

They will mark your passing
like an advent calendar.

I haven't put up
my tree
this year
haven't
hung up my lights,
as though
I already knew
some light
would flicker out.

I didn't know
it would be yours.

There is solace
in the night sky
stars punching out the black
begging light to come through.

There is solace
in the knowledge that
the last time we were in person
I wrapped my arms around you
and told you
I loved you.

Solace in the fact
we celebrate the end
of your life
on the darkest
day of the year.

The Answer
>*For Auntie Terri*

I want rage.
I want to throw the Polish crystal
against the wall,
fall to my knees,
and scream
or sob.

I want my cousin,
my mother,
my younger cousins
to wrap me in their arms.
And at least if not,
to whisper
"Yes. Me too.
Me too. Me too."

I want an explosion.
An outburst.

Any semblance
that this moment
matters more than a moment
at a bedside
when a doctor comes in
after one hundred and twenty minutes
and asks,
"Why are you still here?"

And I say,
"Because until time of death is called,
can we really say they died?"

By which I mean,
I was the only one

willing to stay.

And the nurse said
the doctor would be here soon
and I did not know
soon would take this long.

And – I wasn't sure
when it was appropriate to leave.

And – after a certain point
I just wanted someone to
say the words out loud.

But the rage doesn't come.

There is a small moment in the morning
when my mother meets me in the kitchen
and chants inside my arms,
"I'm all that's left, I'm all that's left."

And I hold her,
the way you hold a screaming infant
that's not yours.

I tuck in my grief.
Swallow the alcohol at ten in the morning,
my cousin laughs and provides.
The beer at night my younger cousin
buys with his own money.

When I think everyone is sleeping,
I sit alone in my dead aunt's room,
watch her belongings disappear,
the drawers empty,
the closet clear except for hangers,
clothing like ghosts.

One night my mother comes in
and finds me drinking and crying alone.

She asks, *"What's wrong?"*

And the fact she asks this question
is the answer.

My Mother's Husband
For Stan Bowker

I was in undergrad, freshmen dorms
when my mom texted me to happily announce her marriage.
I remember the shitty wooden desk I sat at,
eyes wide, shaking my head.

They had only been dating for weeks.

One holiday break, they picked me up from the airport.
I complained the whole drive home about the music.
He tried to step into a parent role and told me
the world does not revolve around me.
When my mother quietly changed the station,
I reminded him, yes, it actually does.

They remained married fifteen years.
My mother is a difficult woman to love.

As time passed, I softened some.
He asked me about my life, my school, my job, my writing.
Slowly, he started answering the phone
when my mother was out,
and we would chat.

Once, my mother told me that
I was the only one out of all the kids
to remember to call on his birthday.

Once, when my cousin stole my blue acoustic guitar,
he found out and mailed out a new one,
fancy case and all.

Once, I decided to give him a gift -
A crappy seven-dollar Target mug that read,

"It's official. You're awesome."
Every time I visited,
He used it.

Only after he's dead do I call him my stepdad.
When he was alive,
I never gave him the chance to call me daughter.

If I Wrote The Obituary Honestly

I would tell you he was in an unhappy marriage for years,
and this likely contributed to his decline.

I would write how my mother would call me to complain
and when I was home, I often had to ask her to be nicer to him.

Once when I hugged him goodbye,
I thanked him for not killing her.
Not because he was abusive,
but because as someone who once lived with her,
I got it.

When we picked up the ashes,
his urn looked like a black plastic trash can.
I told my mom I would upgrade it,
and she said she didn't want to waste the money.

I would write about how even after he is dead,
and the mattress he died on removed from his bedroom,
my mother still insults him.

I would also tell you that though he has children
it took sixteen days
before I was the one to call the funeral home
and ask about the obituary.

The funeral director said he would send a draft
with the notes that he had,
and I would be responsible to fill in "What kind of man he was."

The truth is - I saw him less than once a year,
I don't know what kind of man he was.

If I am being honest,
I would tell you that out of all of the people

my mother dated or married,
he was my favorite,
and he deserved better.

So I wrote the obituary,
because no one else would.

For Brownie

The morning you die,
it's hard to wake up.
The sky is overcast and we
pile into the car.

They'd said because of COVID,
we wouldn't be able to say goodbye,
that we would leave you in a parking lot with strangers,
and go home.

Instead, we are offered a sacrifice,
a garage in exchange for your last breath,
and we take it.

We hold you,
fingertips smoothing out soft skin
as your eyes stop moving,
as your exhale passes through our hands.

The doctor tells us you're already gone,
before we even know it's time.
You went so fast,
no fight left, ready to rest.

She tells us to take our time with your tiny body,
tells us we did our best,
tells us it's okay to say goodbye.

You ride in my lap on the way home,
limp, heavy, muscles twitching as they let go.

And after we bury you,
it rains.

Worst Case Scenario
For PB

The day of his mother's surgery,
I call my partner to ask how it went.

He tells me softly, *It was worst case scenario,*
and I prepare myself for the condolences.

The next week plays through my head-
the funeral preparation,

what dress they'll put her in,
his sisters and grammie sobbing in his arms.

I imagine his father shaking hands with people I don't know,
all of us dressed in black.

They had to break her leg, he says.
It will be a long recovery.

I exhale. *So she's alive then.*
Yes. The funeral stops its procession.

The morning of our boy's surgery,
I'm too tired to get up and see him off.

My partner will go to work later,
I will pick him up after he's awake.

When the doctor calls too soon,
she says she won't sugar coat it.

Says purple tongue and cardiac arrest,
says they tried for as long as they could.

We spend the day robotic - collecting the remains,
allowing those who loved him a small wake,

where he doesn't. And as the sun sets,
we bury him beside his brother.

Alternate Universe Where Your Death Is More Gentle
For Kyla PoopiePants

In this poem, the money does not run out.
I am not forced to find a job,
not trying to save up money.
I can stay home.
I have time to notice the lump
before it becomes marble-sized.
Before the spider web of cancer builds a nest
and spreads like spilled milk.

In this poem, we can do the surgery.
The vet is competent and we find the right meds
so it's safe to be on chemo.

In this poem, we start the treatment sooner.
I do not flinch when they say
it costs nearly $800 a month.
The cancer does not spread through your chest,
create fluid in your lungs, a rasp in your breath.

In this poem, you still die.
But I do not have to leave work early.
I do not scream in my car as I drive home.
You do not bleed into my hands
while my roommate speeds us to the clinic.

Instead, you are just tired.
One night, maybe a year or two from now,
I help you into bed.
You curl up beside me.
We fall asleep together.
And in the morning,
you don't wake up.

Circle 20
Disability

On My Disability

After several minutes of stalemate silence
the man who reeks of alcohol
evaluates my body and asks in disbelief,
"You are disabled? How?"

I want to have him pull up a chair
light a cigarette,
open up a beer,
and brace himself
because most of my therapists
can't even stomach it.

In the span of thirteen seconds,
I want to crack apart my skull
and allow these memories to float like the Milky Way
from my brain, to his.

I want him to see my father, my mother, my brother,
my sister running away, my dog's blood in the driveway,
the bed of a purple truck, the first boy to show me around school
in a car in flames, my sister's best friend in a casket,
my best friend in a casket, several more friends. A near stranger's
bed, the standoff with the mirror, the razor blades,
the nights I wake up screaming, the inability to tell my partner
I love him because the words form a sock in my throat
that is so thick I can barely breathe through.

Instead, the hurricane stays inside me.
I bite my teeth together and
narrow my eyes and
straighten up my spine and say,

"Yes. Would you like to see my paperwork?"

Asking Questions

When my youngest niece sees me in a swimsuit,
she peels various cloth to the side and reads the words
I've painted on my skin.

Three years ago when she was falling asleep,
she'd rubbed my arm.
Her small body stiffened with the question
when she felt the raised flesh
but she didn't ask.

Now they ask.

Now they tell me they love me.

My oldest niece still reaches for my hand
when we walk on beach sand.
'What happened to your arm?' they say.
My mouth falls open.

I try to retch the words out,
try to explain something I'm not sure they'll understand,
until I settle for silence,
because the language I would use
is a gunshot through their little bodies.

How do you tell someone who loves you so much,
they run across parking lots to jump into your arms

that you hate the person they love?

Lemon/Lime

Cabinet is the same as closet is the same as shelf is the same as cat tree is the same as *the place where we put that thing*. Reference is the same as referral is the same as *that other R word I can't think of right now*. Your friend is the same as your sister, your mother, your grammie, *that person you know and like that I can't identify. Give me a second.* A QR Code is *that squiggly thing* and my friend jokes, "Oh my gosh! I do that, too!"

But she doesn't.

Before the accident, I was able to say what I meant to say.

Now, we sit at Denny's.

I order my food,
and the waiter brings me a water with lime.

When I ask why a lime,
the waiter and my roommate confirm,
.... *This is what you ordered.*

And I cry,
because now
lemon is the same as lime.

Circle 21
Continuing To Exist

On Fear

The first time he sees me afraid
we are on a balcony on the ninth floor of a hotel.

There is a cross wind begging to knock
unstable feet off balance
and I am reaching for the guardrail.

He comments on how he's surprised,
that he's never seen me shake as the wind hits,

as the threat of falling sinks into my skin.
The balcony sways in time with my knees.

I want to caution him
it's not the fear of falling

but that sometimes,
I can't trust my feet

to not jump.

Acknowledgements

Dante was Wrong, Maroon Dodge Ram, and *When The News Reads, "School Shooting In Michigan"* were published by Anti Heroin Chick.

Necrophilia was published by Glass - Poets Resist.

When They Become Husbands was published by SWIMM.

Autopsy and *An Ode to the COVID Weight I Gained* were published by Stanchion.

Richmond Park was published with Impspired.

My Body As A Gun was published with SoFloPoJo

Dysmorphia was an Honorable Mention for the Charles Bukowski Poetry Award.

The Perfect Dress was published with Joy of the Pen and received an Honorable Mention for the 2018 Poetry Award.

The New Binary was published with Rise Up Review

What Happens Before You Know Who You Are was published in Frost Meadow Review

Rite of Passage was published in Rat's Ass Review and Frost Meadow Review

Buddy System was published by Sledgehammer.

Resurrection was a finalist for the Beullah Rose Prize and published with Smartish Pace

When You Become a Snowflake was published with Drunk
Monkeys

Winter Solstice won the 2021 River Winter Prize and was
published with Sandy River

For Brownie and *Worst Case Scenario* were both published by
Daily Drunk.

Alternate Universe Where Your Death Is More Gentle was
published by TAB.

The Kind of Man My Father Is
And *Asking Questions* appeared in On Becoming a Role
Model.

Also Available from Stanchion Books

The Woman's Part by Jo Gatford

The House of Skin by Karina Lickorish Quinn

Where We Set Our Easel by Mandira Pattnaik

Irregulars by Kerry Trautman

It Skips a Generation by Alison Lubar

Ghost Mom by T Guzman

UNTENABLE MYSTIC CHARM by travis l. tate

Thoughts I Lost In The Laundry by Leia Butler

Learn more at StanchionZine.com